WACKY COMPARISONS

Wacky Ways to COMPARE SIZE

BY MARK WEAKLAND &
JESSICA GUNDERSON

ILLUSTRATED BY
KEINO, BILL BOLTON, &
IGOR SINKOVEC

capstone
young readers

3 POINTY HUMAN TEETH, it's the truth,

are nearly the length of **1 GREAT WHITE SHARK TOOTH.**

1 shark tooth = 2½ inches (6 centimeters); 1 human tooth = 7/8 in. (22 millimeters)

How many **MARSHMALLOWS** will a hedgehog munch to equal its weight? **120.** That's a bunch!

How long was **APATOSAURUS**, head to tail?

Along its back **30** SKATEBOARDERS sail.

1 apatosaurus = 74 feet (23 meters); 1 skateboard = 2 ft.. 6 in. (76 cm)

1 TARANTULA looking for a meal

fits **15** PENNIES on its back. What a deal!

3.2 MILLION MICE, whisker to tail,

weigh the same as **1** BIG BLUE WHALE.

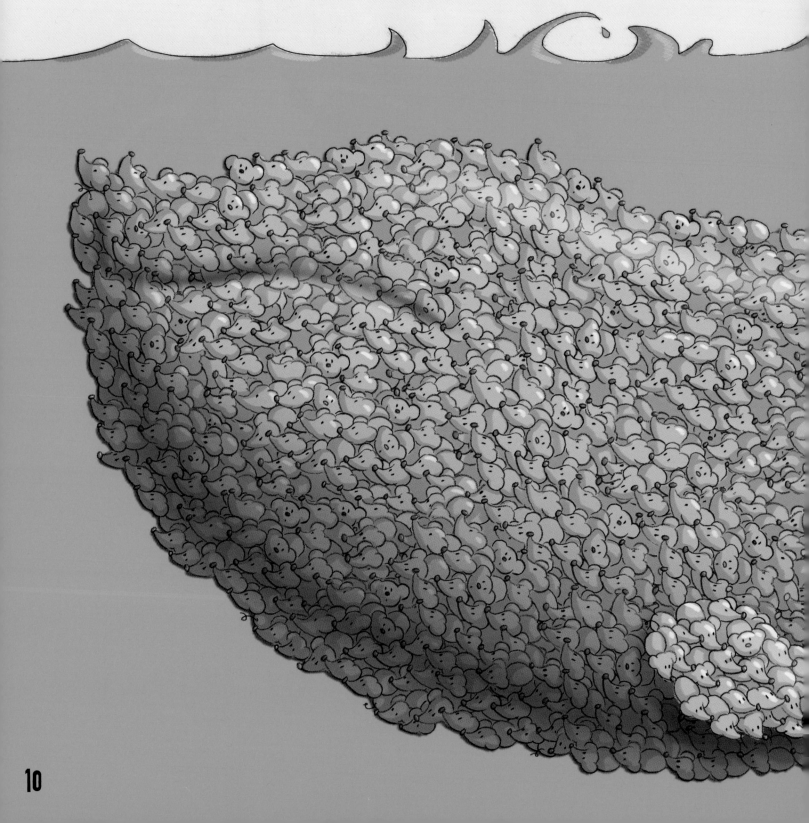

1 whale = 80 tons (73 metric tons); 1 mouse = 0.8 oz. (23 g)

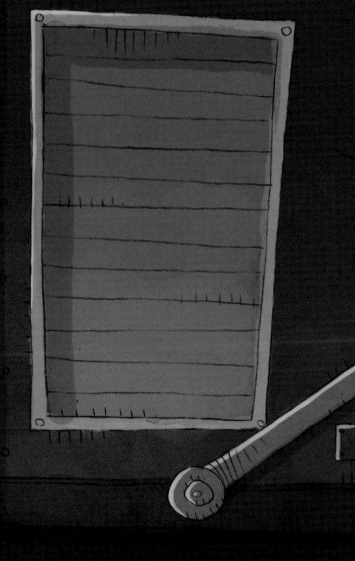

21 SKUNKS, with a little luck,
stand as tall as
1 GARBAGE TRUCK.

64 MINI PRETZELS lined end to end

are as long as **1** OCTOPUS ARM that won't bend.

14

1 arm = 8 ft. (2.4 m); 1 pretzel = 1½ in. (3.8 cm)

"The STATUE OF LIBERTY is tall. It's true!"

say 431 PIGEONS who wobble and coo.

1 statue = 305 ft. (93 m); 1 pigeon = 8½ in. (22 cm)

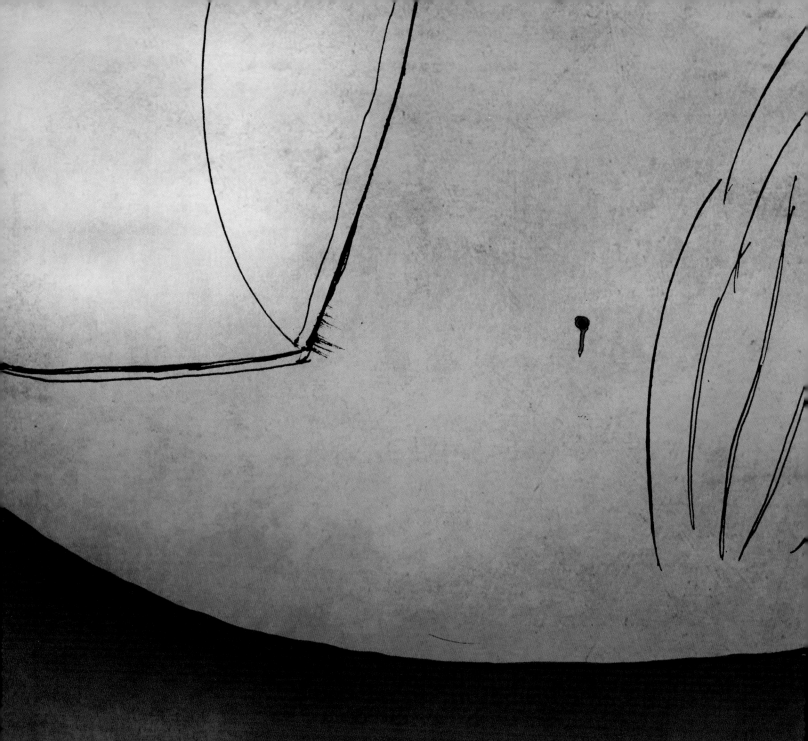

How many **RED BLOOD CELLS** fit inside

1 MOSQUITO'S BELLY that's satisfied?

1 meal = 0.0003 fluid ounces (0.01 milliliters or 10 microliters); 5 million red cells per microliter

50 million

1 OSTRICH, feathered and tall,

1 GLOWING PUMPKIN *in need of braces*

weighs the same as

7 GUINEA PIGS making faces.

1 pumpkin = 15 pounds (6.8 kilograms); 1 guinea pig = 33.5 oz. (950 g)

The world's tallest mountain is
MOUNT EVEREST.

How many ELEPHANTS match

its snowy crest?

2,765

1 mountain = 29,035 ft. (8.8 kilometers); 1 elephant = 10 ft., 6 in. (3.2 m)

To see to the top, we crane our necks.

36 HOT DOGS equal 1 T. REX!

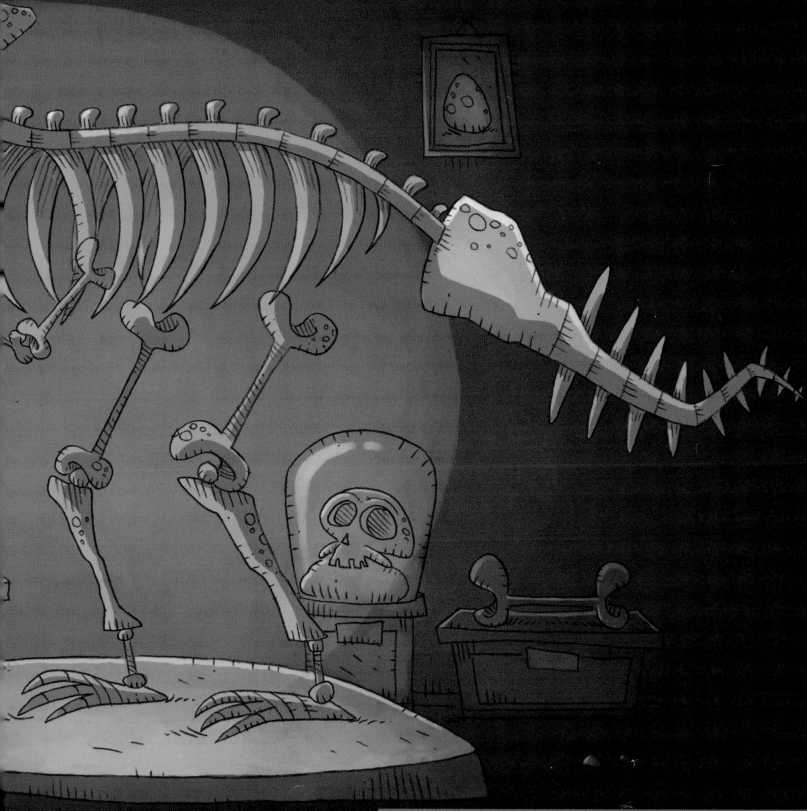

1 T. rex = 18 ft. (5.5 m); 1 hot dog = 6 in. (15 cm)

How much does a **BULLDOZER** weigh?

The same as **19,000 KITTENS** ready to play.

1 bulldozer = 19 tn. (17.2 t); 1 kitten = 2 lb. (907 g)

A ROCKET TO THE MOON is a **3**-DAY RIDE.

How long for a

CAR DRIVING 65?

153 DAYS

(at 65 miles [105 km] per hour)

distance to the moon = 238,855 miles (384,400 km)
rocket speed = 6,635 miles (10,678 km) per hour

READ MORE

Accorsi. William. *How Big Is the Lion?: My First Book of Measuring.* Measure Me! New York: Workman Pub., 2010.

Adamson. Thomas K., and Heather Adamson. *How Do You Measure Length and Distance?* Measure It! Mankato. Minn.: Capstone Press, 2011.

Parker. Vic. *How Heavy Is Heavy?: Comparing Vehicles.* Measuring and Comparing. Chicago: Heinemann Library, 2011.

Vogel. Julia. *Measuring Length.* Mankato. Minn.: The Child's World, 2013.

Special thanks to our adviser, Terry Flaherty, PhD, Professor of English, Minnesota State University, Mankato, for his expertise.

Editor: Jill Kalz
Designer: Ashlee Suker
Art Director: Nathan Gassman
Production Specialist: Eric Manske
The illustrations in this book were created digitally.

Capstone Young Readers are published by Capstone,
1710 Roe Crest Drive, North Mankato, Minnesota 56003
www.capstoneyoungreaders.com

Library of Congress Cataloging-in-Publication Data
Cataloging-in-publication information is on file with the Library of Congress.
ISBN 978-1-62370-037-9

Printed in the United States of America in
North Mankato, Minnesota.
032013   007223CGF13